INTERIOR DESIGN

----- ✤✤✤ -----

THE BEST BEGINNER'S GUIDE FOR NEWBIES

SIMON BRAKE

Copyright 2017 - All rights reserved.

The follow eBook is reproduced below with the goal of providing information that is as accurate and reliable as possible. Regardless, purchasing this eBook can be seen as consent to the fact that both the publisher and the author of this book are in no way experts on the topics discussed within and that any recommendations or suggestions that are made herein are for entertainment purposes only. Professionals should be consulted as needed before undertaking any of the action endorsed herein.

This declaration is deemed fair and valid by both the American Bar Association and the Committee of Publishers Association and is legally binding throughout the United States.

Furthermore, the transmission, duplication or reproduction of any of the following work including specific information will be considered an illegal act irrespective of if it is done electronically or in print. This extends to creating a secondary or tertiary copy of the work or a recorded copy and is only allowed with express written consent of the Publisher. All additional right reserved.

The information in the following pages is broadly considered to be a truthful and accurate account of facts, and as such any inattention, use or misuse of the information in question by the reader will render any resulting actions solely under their purview. There are no scenarios in which the publisher or the original author of this work can be in any fashion deemed liable for any hardship or damages that may befall them after undertaking information described herein.

Additionally, the information in the following pages is intended only for informational purposes and should thus be thought of as universal. As befitting its nature, it is presented without assurance regarding its prolonged validity or interim quality. Trademarks that are mentioned are done without written consent and can in no way be considered an endorsement from the trademark holder.

Table Of Contents

Introduction 1

Chapter 1: Step 1: Principles of Interior Design 7

Chapter 2: Step 2: Finding Your Style 19

Chapter 3: Step 3: Choosing the Perfect Colors 31

Chapter 4: Step 4: Creating Your Budget and Staying on Track 41

Chapter 5: Step 5: Preparing to Decorate 49

Conclusion 59

Introduction

Welcome, and thank you for downloading *Interior Design: The Best Beginner's Guide for Newbies*.

Are you a new homeowner looking to create an interior design that touts a signature style all your own? Or, perhaps it's your current home that needs a facelift. Is that it—is the home where you currently reside in need of a serious makeover? It is likely you answered 'yes' to one of these questions; otherwise, you probably would not be reading a book about interior design, right? Although, I do know some people whose hobby seems to be getting ideas from interior design magazines or books and then taking just a few of those ideas and making some slight changes to their home. Before you know it, your older home has a new personality that gives it a "Better Homes and Garden" appeal.

Once you start learning the principles and techniques presented in our book, you'll be amazed at how just a few inexpensive additions to an otherwise tired décor can be as enjoyable as a million-dollar-makeover. Okay, well perhaps not a million dollar one, but putting some time, effort, and a little money into your home every so often reminds you why you love your home so much.

If you are one who has always considered interior design to be a professional's paradise where the lay person dares not tread, think again! By definition, interior design is the art of

Introduction

planning and executing the design of building interiors and their furnishings. You don't have to be an architect, general contractor with a crew, and it's not necessary to have a degree in the field to improve your home. What you must do is what you are doing now—study the design principles and be prepared to make a few mistakes along the way. That's how you learn; you design a few disasters and hope they are small enough and inexpensive enough to change once your good sense returns.

Studying even just a little about interior design puts you miles ahead when it comes to future remodeling projects. This is one time where a little bit of knowledge isn't dangerous; it's necessary to do before attempting your DIY interior design project. No matter how small or grand your design ideas are, gaining some credible knowledge and creating a proven plan will save you a lot of heartaches.

Most likely you've been giving this interior design idea of yours some serious thought, and you finally feel confident enough to make a commitment to your project. Congratulations, you've taken the first important step that every DIY designer should do. You've decided to do a little research before beginning your design work. Take it from the experts, the time you spend reading through these design principles, learning how to choose the proper colors and add the right amount of texture, and planning an affordable budget that you can stick to will be rewarded with greater satisfaction in your overall design results.

Regardless of how long you have lived in your home, there is a strong possibility you have your eye on a particular look you want to acquire. Whether you saw this dream house look in a magazine or on a home decorating television program, you just can't wrap your mind around how and where to begin.

Novice interior designers can be overwhelming trying to figure out how to turn their dreams into beautiful and functional realities. That's where we come in; this book was written for the specific needs of those wanting to achieve that dream house look but are unsure of how and where to start.

The following chapters are geared toward all the do-it-yourself people just like you, who find themselves with a lot more courage than knowledge when they first entertain the idea of a makeover. There are some things to consider first, and we want you to begin your project with eyes wide open.

Avoid asking for everybody and their brother's opinion of your ideas, especially if they're not professionals. Once you've learned the basic principles, trust your decisions. You'll have an instinct about what looks good and makes you feel good about the changes you plan on making.

Don't be afraid to challenge yourself, but if you get a gut feeling that you've gone to radical, you probably have. As a newbie, it's better to play it safe with the things that are too costly to change. Keep your bigger, more expensive items rather neutral, so if your choice is too bold, it won't break the bank to modify it. If your floor feels too blah, you can always add interest and color with an area rug. If your walls are too neutral, you can always add accent colors and textures in your furnishings to give it that designer flair.

If your personality is bold and outgoing, you might want to tone it down in your design. Your ideas are going to complement your personality, but they shouldn't be at the expense of making others feel comfortable and welcomed. On the other hand, if your personality is rather introverted, realize that the bolder colors, objects, and architectural features are always going to make you feel like you're stepping out on a

Introduction

limb over the Grand Canyon. In this case, you might want to bring in a trusted friend to ask for his or her opinion. Make it a person who perhaps has a bit more confidence or is a little braver than you when it comes to change.

Expect to make some mistakes along the way, that's part of the DIY fun and frustration. A little further on in this book we're going to discuss planning and committing to a budget, but you will need to build in a cushion in case of a mistake or two in the design process.

Don't try to please everybody; do what makes you and your family feel comfortable and happy. If your mother or best friend don't find your design changes to their liking, it's time for you just to say NEXT! This is the time to express your personality and taste and find your style. If you don't explore the possibilities in color, texture, and incorporating some different styles to determine what pleases you, there's little chance that you'll ever feel safe enough to experiment with another interior design project. The people who are living in the house and yourself should be the ones your design serves.

Don't listen to those who tell you that you can count on spending double what you've budgeted for in your design project. Wrong! We're going to teach you to set a proper budget, commit to sticking to that budget, and manage your purchases and changes to your plan while still staying within that budget. There's no use in having a budget that you plan to exceed on the outset. You can create a beautiful design and still be on budget and on time, but it takes discipline and sometimes saying "no" to your first choice. When you find that perfect look, but it doesn't have an excellent price, then shop around until you find something better. You'll be more than pleased and feel even better about your choices when you didn't have to break the bank to get the look you want.

DIY interior design projects are all about shopping bargains. Isn't it true, that if you could have afforded the best of the best, you probably would have hired a professional? There's no shame in negotiating and knowing when to limit yourself to what you need over what you want. Plan on compromises along the way instead of spending double your budget.

Honestly, when given the right tools and guidance, anyone can be do-it-yourself savvy. These chapters will cover the steps one should take when venturing into interior design. Included in these pages, you will find the basic principles of interior design, choosing the perfect colors and style for your home, staying on top of your budget, and bringing the completed project together to achieve just the look you wanted. By the time you are through reading our book, you should be feeling very confident about beginning your very own adventure in interior design.

Chapter 1:

Step 1: Principles of Interior Design

Embarking on any home improvement project can be scary and overwhelming, and that's why many potentially talented DIY designers never see their dreams come to fruition. You may have watched a few home improvement programs on television, seen weekend warriors duke it out over costly mistakes or unexpected problems that crop up right in the middle of their design projects.

To give you a small bit of reassurance, know that many of the people who attempt to do DIY design projects are also under the impression that they can do all the work themselves. Hollywood loves the drama these projects foster, and so all their issues get played out over a national audience. By their own admittance, most of them have never renovated before, and yet they're planning to renovate their entire kitchen in three days. They've somehow convinced themselves they are electricians, plumbers, carpenters, architects, and designers. These are the ideas that make better viewing on television than in completed projects.

Chapter 1 – Step 1: Principles of Interior Design

Keep in mind the definition of interior design. It's the art of planning and executing, which doesn't mean you need to be all things to all people. As you get further into the book, you'll realize the things you can do well and those things that are beyond your scope. If you make your first interior design project a lesson in frustration, you'll spoil the excitement of seeing your design come to life. All you'll remember is that your DIY design project was a giant headache. The operative word in the definition of interior design is "PLANNING." You cannot properly execute a plan you don't have!

You're right to worry in the beginning. It can be a real challenge discovering just how to start planning your design, especially if you are not familiar with the details of the project. Knowing which steps to take when will provide some direction, but taking our step-by-step process will ease your mind and soon give you the confidence of a professional. The best place to start is with our basic principles of interior design. The following chapter will cover these basic principles and give you a head start on your design project.

These valuable fundamentals will enable you to navigate your way through all the challenges when designing and creating the home of your dreams. Our principles have been proven effective by professional interior designers, so you'll be in good company as you progress through this first design. Consider the steps to be your map to successful design ideas and strategies. Once you get comfortable and more confident, you'll be adding all those special touches that will make your home unique. Not everyone has the same vision, wants, or needs for their home, so don't fret if some of the steps and principles do not pertain to your project.

Each time you deviate from the recommended step, you're putting your style and flavor to the home. Some steps have no option but to follow, such as creating and committing to a budget. Stepping outside your budget won't give flavor to your home; it could end your interior design project altogether.

Okay, let's examine the principles of interior design so that your success won't be by accident but by design.

Emphasis

In interior design, the emphasis is the point of interest or the focal point of a room. When you walk into a room, you should immediately be able to tell the purpose and personality of the room. As your eyes float across the room's features, you'll notice one prominent element. This is known as the focal point; it's where your eye hesitates before absorbing all the beauty, textures, and colors within the room.

While it's important to design an attention-grabbing focal point, if you create too many elements to catch the eye it can make your room unappealing and somewhat confusing. It's like reading a book with no plot and too many characters; it has the potential to be interesting, but finding your way through the maze is just too taxing. The same holds true with designs that could look beautiful, but there's something about them that makes you uncomfortable. The colors could be off, the textures could be flat, but in most cases, it begins and ends with no focal point or too many.

Choosing every element carefully to go well with the entire room and leave a lasting impression on your visitors is paramount to great design. Unfortunately, the mistake many newbies make is that they have too many outstanding elements with nothing to make one hesitate and take in the

Chapter 1 – Step 1: Principles of Interior Design

beauty of how that one object claims the room. If this happens, you've missed the point—the focal point you needed to add to the room for emphasis. There are two types of emphasis.

Architectural Emphasis

Architectural emphasis is when you choose to utilize a structural feature as the focal point.

- Fireplaces and large windows are examples of architectural features.

- Design the whole room around this feature.

- Decorating large windows with elements such as curtains or valances, and fireplaces with items of interest can add just the right amount of architectural emphasis.

Piece Emphasis

Piece emphasis is not a focal point that is built into the home as an architectural emphasis is, but rather accomplished with a showcased object. Piece emphasis is when you add a particular feature to the room and design around it. Antiques, a specific piece of furniture, artwork and high ceilings are a few examples of piece emphasis. Adding a spotlight to the artwork or the particular piece of furniture can help draw more attention to it. Adding a chandelier to a high ceiling is an excellent way to add emphasis.

Rhythm

Rhythm is color patterns, different shapes, and prints that will influence the course your eyes take. Rhythm consists of four different methods: alternation, repetition, contrast and progression.

Alternation is alternating two or more elements. You can achieve this look by alternating the items of your choice in a pattern that will influence the direction of your vision. The following photo illustrates the use of alternation on the stairs, encouraging you to lift your gaze upward with each step. Alternation also offers interest and excitement in your design, lending a pleasing enthusiasm to follow its direction.

Chapter 1 – Step 1: Principles of Interior Design

Repetition is repeating elements such as colors, patterns, or textures throughout the space. You can achieve this look by matching the color of one item in the room with another item in the same area. An example could be matching the rug or carpet in your room with the drapes or valance. You can also create repetition in objects. It's most common to repeat in threes or fives when adding objects to shelves or walls for balance. Repetition adds weight to your space as well, so make sure that you haven't unintentionally created too many focal points by overusing repetition.

Contrast is when you put two or more elements in opposition to each other. An example of this would be using opposing colors such as white and black or different shapes such as circles and squares. Contrast and repetition go together, but they can battle for the position of importance if you use too much of one and not enough of the other. The stronger the contrast, the more you should think about softening its effect

Interior Design

so as not to turn your field of difference into a steady stream of more of the same. For example, if you decide to do a black and white tile floor in a bathroom, softening the colors of the tile will still offer contrast but will help it not to look like a 1950s dinner. In the illustration below, notice how the print on the area rug is broken up by the three large ottomans is a soft leather.

Progression is the gradual decrease or increase of an object or element by color or size. One way to do this would be to use objects that are slightly different shades of the same color. Another way is by using objects such as vases or candles but gently graduate their sizes. A word of caution, avoid using too much progression or on many larger objects, or your room will begin to look as though it's listing to one side.

Harmony and Unity

Creating harmony and unity in your home can be a challenge for the novice decorator; it's a big undertaking to make sure all the elements in the rooms of your home flow nicely together without clashing. Of course, you can use your hallways as

Chapter 1 – Step 1: Principles of Interior Design

natural transitions between rooms, which makes it easier to blend the elements you are incorporating. Be sure to consider décor and furniture as well, and keep it simple. Less is best! Give the visitor's eye time to travel from one element to another without having to hurdle heavy furniture or crowded elements. These are the details that will prevent your walls and furnishings from appearing too busy.

Here are some ways to help achieve harmony and unity throughout the spaces of your home.

- Have similar color schemes (this helps make the transition from room to room as smooth as possible)
- Install the same or similar flooring in all rooms
- Design with coinciding textures and shapes
- Apply patterns consistently throughout your home
- Decorate with items that are theme appropriate

Proportion and Scale

Proportion and scale relate to the size of and ratio between your design elements. Deciding what size pieces to use in your rooms will depend on the actual size of the space, as well as the height of the windows and ceiling. The following tips will help you choose appealing design elements.

- Use the largest furniture and décor in your larger rooms.
- Place smaller elements in your smaller rooms.
- Taller furniture goes well in rooms with high ceilings.

Avoid using design objects or accessories that are all at eye level. By using objects and furnishing of different sizes and heights, you encourage the eye to navigate and flow rather than merely skimming the space.

Balance

Balance is the equal placement of visual weight in a room. Having balance in a room makes you feel more comfortable and relaxed because it's more aesthetically pleasing. There are three different types of balance in interior design, symmetrical balance, asymmetrical balance and radial balance.

Symmetrical balance is when objects are mirrored or repeated on a central axis. This type of balance is more traditional and can easily be achieved. For example, if you have an end table and lamp on one side of the couch, you would have the same end table and lamp on the other side of the sofa. Using symmetrical balance can also help you to avoid making one side of the room heavily weighted, and the other side seems somewhat bare. Find your focal point and build your designs evenly on each side of that element.

Chapter 1 – Step 1: Principles of Interior Design

Asymmetrical balance is when different objects of equal visual weight are placed on either side of an axis. It is very casual and has more variety but is also more challenging to achieve. An example would be to place two of the same size chairs across from a couch. The challenge comes when color or pattern adds weight and texture to the furniture, making it appear larger or heavier than your match. When this happens, a quick fix is to add a few pillows for balance.

Interior Design

Radial balance or radial symmetry is when objects are arranged around a center point. These objects usually extend inward or outward from the center point. An example of this would be a circular table with chairs positioned around it. To create radial symmetry in a kitchen, you might have a large island with a sink or stove in the center. To balance the island in the room, add some bar stools on the opposite side. Radial balance is achieved with the weight of the sink or stove on one side of the island and the bar stools on the other.

When working with radial symmetry, notice that your design might have blank spacing toward the outside of the room or object. If you find this is the case with your room, just place a plant or a corner curial for balance and interest.

Chapter 1 – Step 1: Principles of Interior Design

The success of your designs will depend on how well you apply these principles, so take a few moments to review them. Learn what creates emphasis and interest. Examine the difference in emphasis to discover if there is one that you find more appealing. You should now have a good understanding of the basic principles of interior design. With the help of these fundamentals, you are ready to hone in on the design aspect of your project.

Chapter 2:

Step 2: Finding Your Style

When beginning your interior design project, the first thing to consider is what style you wish to achieve. Most beginners already have a clear idea of what appeals to them, of styles they have seen in the past that they found inviting and welcoming. To discover your style, you can do the following. It's not essential that you know the names of the styles you prefer, just keep the picture of those designs in your head to refer to later.

Think of a friend's home that you find especially pleasing. Now picture your favorite room in that home and ask yourself the following questions.

- What is the color?
- As you picture the room, what is its focal point or emphasis?
- Are the furnishings light and airy, or does the room have a lot of darker woods and furniture?
- Would you say it has smooth, clean lines, or is it earthy in appearance?
- What is it about this room that you find memorable?

Chapter 2 – Step 2: Finding Your Style

- Could you see yourself relaxing in a similar room if you incorporated this look in your home?

Without realizing it before, you probably sensed the balance and harmony in the room. Balance and harmony is created by the designer's style and the elements they chose to portray that style. Interior design novices often believe that they must use the same style throughout the home, but this is not necessarily true. Although you want the elements to be in harmony, that doesn't mean you must use the same style from foyer to family room. Instead, you might choose to blend two entirely different styles like contemporary and rustic.

It's a little more work to make sure the styles transition and blend well and that you have created harmony, but there's a way to test your design and to ensure you have accomplished your desired effect. If you are blending two styles, it's a good idea to make one your primary design style and include the other as a secondary, less dominant look that compliments the main design style.

For example, if you decide that you want your DIY design to be contemporary style with a blend of classic, then keep the colors in the pastel pallet and the furniture clean, but add a bit more boldness in your accents and accessories. Before deciding which style or styles to choose, consider these three questions.

1. Will this style go well with the entire house?

2. Is this style appropriate for this specific room?

3. Does this style reflect my personality and preferences?

Now that you have considered these questions, we can begin learning about some of the different styles. Decorating styles can be as diverse and varied as those designing the interiors, but this chapter will only be discussing a few. Feel free to broaden your horizons and research more about the other style designs as you gain experience and confidence.

Classic

If you're the "pull-off-your-boots by the fire" kind of person, then the classic style is most likely going to make you feel like a fish out of water. Classic style has a sophisticated and elegant feel that was inspired by artists from ancient Greece and Rome. Its formal look appeals to people who like everything in its proper place, with luxurious accents and more sculpted lines. If you prefer the classic style, be aware that it can often be overdone, resulting in a rather vulgar display of over-the-top, palace-like golden and heavily sculpted furniture, artwork, and mirrors. Keep in mind; classic should be classy. Even though the furniture and features are formal, avoid the busyness of too many pieces with curls and swirls.

The classic style uses symmetrical balance, as well as metal, glass, and marble accents. Some of the furniture includes grand chandeliers and oversized architectural pieces set off by elegant fabrics like velvet, satin, and silk to give texture and emphasis to the home. Crown moldings, paneled walls, and try ceilings add to the classic design, all the while giving the eye plenty of space to wander both vertically and horizontally.

Color also plays an important part in the classic design, using soft, neutral shades such as light pastels and cool blends as you move from one room to another. If not attentive to your design, the classic style can tend to look a bit feminine, so if

Chapter 2 – Step 2: Finding Your Style

you're designing the room with a man in mind but love the classic style, be sure to "man up" with some of the elements you add to the room.

Modern

Modern style is known for being very simple and free of clutter, sophisticated and classy. As a new designer, be sure to avoid the appearance of coldness. This can be done with area rugs and a few heavier pieces placed strategically in the room. Darker stains on wooden floors also give your modern design a bit more warmth and energy. Another feature that can give your room a welcoming sense of intimacy to the modern style is lighting. A combination of natural light that brightens the entire room and artificial lighting to shine over a piece of art will give the room that "come hither" look.

Let your colors and textures add a cozy touch to your design. The modern style includes straight line designs that implement geometric shapes that complement high ceilings and bare windows. Many times, in the modern style, windows are left free of coverings to allow the sunlight to showcase your design. For privacy, you might decide on a clean, easy-to-operate shade that lowers over the windows at night.

The furniture in modern décor is typically minimal but can be bold in color. If you decide to incorporate metal into your modern design for texture, be sure to contrast it with a cushy piece for balance. Because of the free lines in the modern style, it is easier to add to your design—so, again, keep it simple. You'll see what you need to add when you hang your artwork and place a few pieces for color and balance.

The flooring tends to be wood or tile, but rugs are sometimes added for a pop of color or warmth. If you choose to use tile, which again can add to the coldness of the modern style, you'll want your rugs to be plush and colorful. The modern style is excellent if you're a no-frills kind of person. Piece emphasis such as sculptures and artwork are usually the focal point in modern style.

Chapter 2 – Step 2: Finding Your Style

Contemporary

Contemporary style is like modern style with a few slight but obvious differences. Contemporary style is known for being more welcoming and appealing to the eye. Like the modern style, contemporary style is also free of excess clutter and uses smooth, clean lines that are a bit more trendy in design and geometric shapes that catch the eye of those that favor a modern style with a cozier feel. Like the more modern style, contemporary designs bend to the neutral colors but use accents in bright and bold colors to make the room pop.

Furniture tends to be neutral tones and is simple and uncluttered. Adding bold accessories along with splashes of color can help liven up the furniture and give the room more interest and excitement. You will not find skirts that cover bulky legs on contemporary furniture; it is most often lifted off the floor to give it that airy, sleek feel. Although the contemporary style incorporates a lot of leather in their furniture, it is often crafted in the lighter and creamier shades to continue with that smooth feel of which the contemporary style is so noted. There aren't too many "middle of the fence" people when it comes to contemporary; you either love it or hate it.

If you're trying to achieve that industrial style in a room with low ceilings and closed off rooms, it might be a challenge. You need the space to pull it off to perfection. In these cases, combining the rustic style with some steampunk pieces can give the same feel in a fraction of the space.

The floors are usually wood, tile, or vinyl, just like the modern style, but the area rugs pull out those bold colors and graphic patterns from your added accessories. When you carry out the geometric patterns in your rugs as well, the room suddenly comes alive with palpable texture.

Industrial

Industrial style has a warehouse type look and feel to it, with many of today's designers incorporating that steampunk spirit of fun and youthful flavor. It is full of raw, unfinished textures with rough, unfinished surfaces and exposed pipes holding the line in the elements of industrial design.

Natural brick walls or brick facing can also be used to pull together the entire storehouse feel. The industrial style maximizes its use of open space, both horizontally and vertically, with rooms unencumbered by walls and ceilings that extend far higher than most, many of which incorporate the HVAC pipes into the design, drawing the eye to the massive vertical expanses of the industrial design.

When you're attempting to get the true industrial look in a room with lower ceilings and smaller, divided rooms, it can be quite the challenge. Combining some steampunk features with

Chapter 2 – Step 2: Finding Your Style

a more rustic design might give you enough of the industrial feel to satisfy your craving for that warehouse feel.

Like several of the other designs, the flooring tends to be wood as well but not the smooth, finished wood used in the other styles. Industrial wooden floors have that barn wood quality that makes you feel as though you just stepped back into the 1800s. For those who love nostalgia, the industrial style takes you there.

Traditional

Unlike any other, the traditional style is elegant, homey, and formal. It has a very calm and classic feel about it and uses a great deal of symmetry. Everything has its place in the traditional style, as you complete the room with predictable perfection. Traditionalists aren't fond of surprises, so you will rarely see modern style mixed with the traditional look—no wild splashes of bold neon colors should adorn a traditional space.

The furniture and art pieces are consistent and match to add balance. Most of the furnishings tend to come in pairs and are centered in both the room and on the windows and shelves. Traditional style uses both horizontal and vertical lines, so the eye stays centered as well. Colors that are not too dark or too light are found in traditional style, along with muted floral prints and carefully placed pillows of matching color and shape.

Window coverings are typically pleated drapes backed by creamy sheers to give warm and support the room's calm appearance. It's acceptable to add a valance that matches the muted florals in the room but keep the colors more monotone and casual. The entire room should speak to your family values and invite a gathering of all the relatives for a comfortable evening of lounging relaxation.

Flooring tends to be wood or vinyl, and often in the darker and richer stains to match the woods used in the furniture. The wooden pieces are often made of maple, mahogany, and the deep red tones of cherry to create a space that appeals to today's family but remembers yesterday's traditions.

Chapter 2 – Step 2: Finding Your Style

Rustic

Rustic style is comfortable and charming, with yesterday's memories and warmth. It uses wide open space and natural elements that are casually placed in interesting nooks and alcoves. The rustic style lends itself well to thematic design, wrapping itself around pieces of the "old West" or the old-world charm of a Tuscan village. Its colors are the rich greens, reds, and browns of earthy vegetables and fruits that you'd find growing in the fields, and its accent pieces could be some of the tools used to turn those fields. Although it has a specific design, the rustic style can appear to be pieces and furniture that has been left over for ages and brought into the space for sentiment and nostalgia.

Large windows are used to create a sense of being closer to nature, as the designer brings the outside inside. You'll often see natural stone fireplaces that travel from floor to ceiling, sporting bulky raw mantles that display large brass lanterns in rustic decorating. Natural, woven fabrics are used in colors and textures that are warm and earthy. Floors tend to be made of natural wood, giving the home a welcoming tone for the family to gather.

No matter what style you use, be consistent with your pieces, colors, and textures. It's okay to combine ones that are compatible such as modern and contemporary, but err on the side of conservative when it comes to trying to be bold and different. Always keep in mind, for any newbie just beginning to spread their designer wings, less is more. If you are planning on incorporating some pieces of a different style, make sure they are in relatable styles, like classic and traditional, or rustic and industrial. Putting classic pieces in an industrial style would compromise the integrity of your design.

Most importantly, make sure your design reflects your personality and taste. Don't design to please the professional, design to please yourself. If there are challenging architectural or construction changes that need to be made, consult the professionals. Don't try to wear too many hats. Be the designer and let others more experienced complete the behind the scenes necessities.

Chapter 2 – Step 2: Finding Your Style

If you're not in love with your design from the start, you'll never be entirely satisfied with your accomplishment. Time does not make the heart grow fonder when it comes to design. Instead, time tends to make your eye stop on the items or issues that frustrate you, so change it until you fall in love with your space instead of settling for a room that didn't turn out as expected. If there's something about the room that bothers you, but you can't put your finger on the problem, go on a search and rescue mission. Move things around, add or remove pieces that always seem to be the topic of your concerns. You're no different than many professionals; even the professionals don't always get it right the first time. Designing for newbies is a work in progress, but, in the end, you should be pleased with your results.

Chapter 3:

Step 3: Choosing the Perfect Colors

You should now have a good idea of what interior design is and its basic principles. With these basic principles in your designer toolbox, let's talk color. A quick, easy, and affordable way to make an immediate change to a room is by altering its color. While interior design is full of different elements, color tends to be the most pleasurable.

There are probably a million thoughts running through your head. Thoughts such as, "What if I don't like the color?' or "What if the colors don't look good together or match with the rest of the house?" Choosing color does not have to be a stressful experience. The good news is, if you know much about each color and related color schemes, it can be an extremely rewarding experience.

First, you should know a little about the color wheel. Colors are grouped on the color wheel, so it's a good idea to familiarize yourself with these groupings:

Complementary Colors

Complementary colors are those that are on opposite sides of each other on the color wheel. For example, red's

Chapter 3 – Step 3: Choosing the Perfect Colors

complimentary color is green. When using complementary colors in their full hue, be careful not to make it too jarring or vibrant for the space and its design. You can mute the hues for a softer, more relaxing feel and still use the colors that complement one another. These complementary colors are typically used to give a feature prominence, but using them in a large space can be overwhelming.

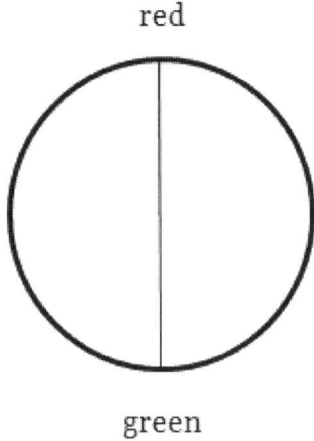

Analogous Colors

Analogous colors are the colors right next to each other on the color wheel. The analogous colors are those most frequently found in nature, and they create that natural harmony when used in a room. The challenges of using analogous colors are to create enough contrast to prevent one color from just melting into the next. If you keep the following three rules in mind, you will experience success when using analogous colors.

Rule #1: Make one of your analogous colors dominant.

Rule #2: Use your second analogous color to support the dominant one.

Rule #3: Couple, your third analogous color with gray, white, or black, to be used as an accent.

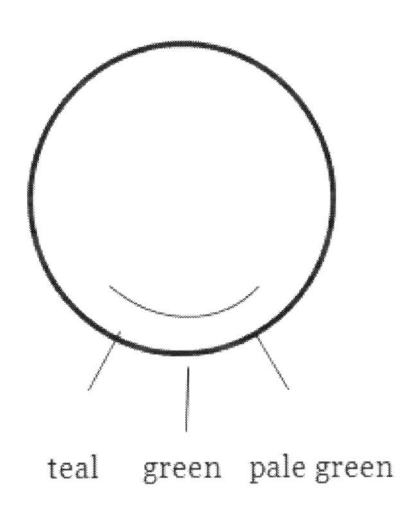

teal   green   pale green

Triad Colors

The triad color scheme implements those colors that are spaced evenly throughout the wheel. They tend to be quite vibrant, so the rules for using triad colors are a bit different.

Rule #1: Make one of your triad colors dominant.

Rule #2: Make your second and third colors accents for support

Rule #3: Use muted hues to create more relaxation in your design.

Chapter 3 – Step 3: Choosing the Perfect Colors

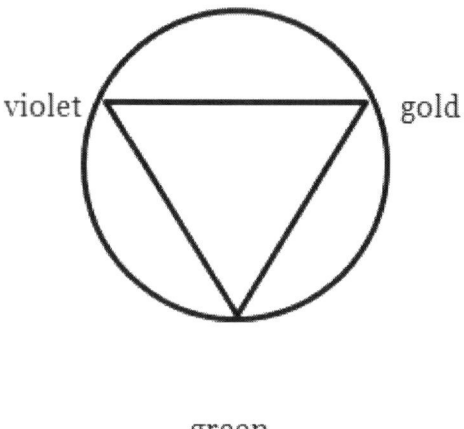

violet

gold

green

Split Complementary Colors

This color scheme resembles the complementary color scheme; only it is split into three colors instead of two. If you were to use one of your base colors in the complementary color scheme as red, then you would split that and use the color to the right which is orange and the color to the left which is pale violet. Your third base would be green, the same as in your complementary colors. The split complementary color scheme is much easier for novice designers to use because it's not overly vibrant, and it's easier to transition.

Interior Design

pale violet — orange

green

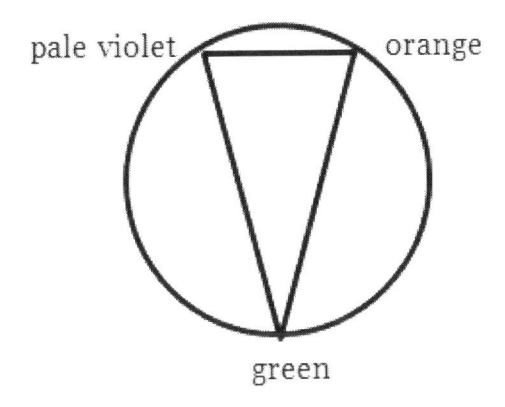

Rectangle (Tetradic) Colors

These also play off the complementary colors, only they use four colors instead of two, and they are in pairs. Designers use the rectangle color scheme when they want lots or opportunity to add color variations to their designs. The rules for using this color scheme are as follows.

Rule #1: Make one color the dominant color in your design.

Rule #2: Use the other three colors to as support in your accent features.

Rule #3: Maintain a balance between cooler and warmer tones in your chosen colors.

Chapter 3 – Step 3: Choosing the Perfect Colors

red

pale orange

light blue

green

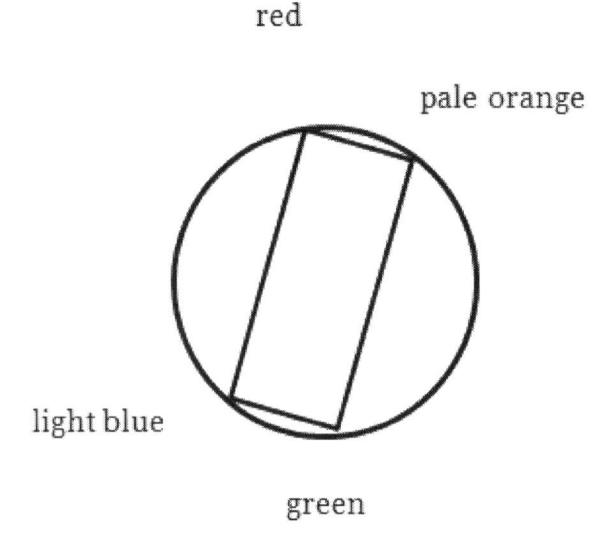

Square Colors

This color scheme is much like the rectangle scheme, as it makes use of four colors. The difference is that the four colors used are evenly spaced around the color wheel. The rules are the same as in the rectangle scheme.

There are different aspects of choosing colors that people enjoy. Some take pleasure in picking a few colors and using them throughout their entire home. Some want to have bold, bright colors as accents, and still, others choose to keep it simple with warmer, neutral colors. Whatever your preference, be sure it matches your design. For example, you wouldn't use bold colors with a classic design. On the other hand, you would want some vibrant colors as accents in a contemporary design. It's all about balance and personal taste. If you stick to the few fundamental rules when blending colors, you'll be sure to apply a color pallet that is both pleasing and properly suites your chosen style.

A little tip when choosing colors—HAVE FUN! Experiment with different colors, and choose what makes you feel like coming home. Now that we've introduced you to the different color schemes, it's time we discussed color. Colors give life to your designs, and how they are used reflects your personality, impacts and emphasizes the pieces your choose in your design, and even influences your thoughts and mood as you relax and enjoy your creation.

One of the most important things is to choose colors that will achieve the look and feel you want when entering a room. Give yourself time to examine the colors you believe will have a positive effect on you, your family, and your guests. Also, make sure the colors are appropriate for that specific room and its design. Picking out happy colors for rooms you entertain in will make the room feel bright and warm. When choosing your colors, remember that lighter shades make the room feel bigger and brighter, while darker shades encourage feelings of cozy intimacy.

Deciding to apply warm colors or cool colors is another challenging part of choosing your color scheme. Colors such as blue, green and purple are considered cool colors. Warm colors are the reds, yellows, and oranges. Evenly mixing cool and warm colors can give your room an undecided inconsistency and a space that is not harmonious, so once you've decided what is best for the room, stick with one color as the dominant one and use the others colors in your wheel in a supportive role with your accent pieces.

Knowing what kind of lighting you have in each room can also be a deciding factor when it comes to the colors you choose. Rooms with a great deal of sunlight would look great with a cooler color scheme. After all, you don't want to the room to look hot—you want it to be welcoming. If a room does not get

Chapter 3 – Step 3: Choosing the Perfect Colors

much sunlight, a warmer color can help brighten it. Let's take a closer look at some of the different color choices and the effects they can have.

Neutrals (black, white, brown, and gray)

Neutrals work well in any room. They blend with every color, and they are classic, stylish, subtle and remarkably flexible. They can help to tone down overpowering colors as well as add depth to a room. Neutrals are a great choice if you are using piece emphasis such as an accent wall. This will make your piece the center of attention, and help your architectural features stand out.

Blues

Depending on the shade you choose, blue can be a calming and relaxing color. Lighter blues are known to have a calming effect, and can even slow your breathing as well as lower blood pressure. Choosing a bright shade of blue and using it in a room with a great deal of sunlight is a way to achieve a calming effect. These shades of blue are commonly used in bathrooms and bedrooms. Darker blues tend to have a negative effect. Dark shades of blue can cause a feeling of sadness, so it is not recommended as a primary color choice.

Purples

Purple is known as a sophisticated and dramatic color, but lighter shades can have the same calming effect as brighter shades of blue. If you want to go for a more sophisticated look, using a dark shade of purple is an excellent choice. Just be sure to incorporate some bright, neutral elements; otherwise, you could mistakenly create a sad and depressing room as you would with the darker shades of blue.

Greens

Green is warm and comforting, yet cool and relaxing. It's a happy color, known to relieve stress and give you and guests positive feelings of finally coming home. It is appealing to the eye and can give one a sense of harmony and peace. Green is commonly utilized in bedrooms and even family rooms to create a natural peace and restful environment.

Yellows

Yellow is a fun, happy color that can brighten a room and bring it to life. It is a very uplifting and energetic color. Yellow is commonly used in bathrooms and kitchens.

Oranges

Orange is a very high energy and exciting color. It can unleash anxieties, which make it a great color for a child's playroom or an exercise space. You can easily tone the color down by adding a few neutral elements.

Reds

Like orange, red is a very intense, high-energy color. Its warmth promotes hunger and brings people together for great conversation. This makes red an excellent choice of color for a kitchen or family room. Be aware that red can also bring out aggression, so tone it down by incorporating some neutral elements.

Now you have an idea of some of the basic colors and how they can affect the overall look of a room. Another thing to be aware of when choosing colors is lighting. Light plays a vital role because it can make colors look different depending on the type. Be sure to test your color choices with samples

Chapter 3 – Step 3: Choosing the Perfect Colors

before painting the entire room. When checking your color and lighting, use the type of light that will be used the most in that specific room. For example, natural light and artificial light. Lighting can make or break your color, so be sure you are checking.

Chapter 4:

Step 4: Creating Your Budget and Staying on Track

It would be amazing to have unlimited resources for your designs, but for most of us, budget drives everything from architectural changes, professional assistance with the changes you want to make, and the accent pieces you use to emphasize style. It's a balance between what you want, what you need, and the compromises required to stay on budget. What you'll find as you get experience in the wonderful world of design is that some of those compromises are quite fun and end up giving you a unique look for a fraction of the cost.

You've probably looked at those Hollywood designs and thought you could never duplicate them on your budget, right? First of all, part of the thrill of design is doing your own thing in your décor, but on the other side is doing your think while shopping for bargains and implementing special features that you may never have tried if you had more money to spend.

For example, you may have used expensive glass backsplash in the kitchen if money was no object. When budget required you to move to plan B, you used broken glass pieces mixed in epoxy and gave your backsplash a one-of-a-kind artistic look that stayed well within your budget. You'll find that those

Chapter 4 – Step 4: Creating Your Budget and Staying on Track

artistic touches you give your design because you didn't have the money in your budget to purchase your first choice are the very things you'll get the most compliments on when people come to visit. Everybody appreciates that unique style you can call your own.

Regardless if you are redecorating a newer or older home, it is nice to be able to cut back where you can. Before considering a budget, go through your home and write down what you want to add or change. First, you should consider what major projects you would like to cover in your budget. A few of the more popular and more expensive ones include:

- Kitchen renovations
- Basement makeovers
- Bathroom additions or makeovers
- Family Room redesigns

When choosing which rooms to include in your makeovers with the amount of money you have allotted yourself to spend, consider in which of those rooms you spend the most time. Sometimes it's a matter of need—which room needs the most repair or requires updates that will make your home easier to sell when you need to attract more buyers for an up-and-coming move.

Speaking of updating or designing with a move in mind, this is a good time to discuss how that will affect your design decisions. Depending on your location, there are certain design styles that appeal to a broader range of potential buyers, so take that into consideration when you chose your design. Hopefully, you haven't lived in an outdated, no-style home for years, only to decide to put money in it when you move. What a shame to miss out on all the rewards and wonderful feeling you get when you create a beautiful space for you and your family.

It's surprising how many people chose to let their home go, living with the frustrations of needed repairs and improvements, and then make it beautiful for those who live there after they leave. Treat yourself to the fun and fantasy of living in your dream space. Even if your home isn't the place you would choose to live if you had more money, it's possible to make it look like a million bucks. Take pride in your place, and make your space sensational. You live in the present, so live as though you were going to stay in this home forever and give it the loving touches that make you feel proud and comfortable.

Believe it or not, with proper planning and knowing where to shop for bargains, as well as having an eye for the fundamental styles we have presented to you in this book; you can turn drab into dreamy. With a little imagination, inexpensive features can look as rich and luxurious as the more expensive items, and usually they're a lot more interesting and rewarding to create.

When you're organizing, and prioritizing your design budget, another aspect that can be of great assistance is factoring in the size of the rooms you are planning to redo and how much remodeling you anticipate. Obviously, there will probably be some elements in your design that you're going to need help with to achieve a professional look. Be sure to figure adequate professional assistance into your budget for the challenges that might just get the best of you. It's no fun to run up against a problem you can't handle, and have nothing left in the budget to get the work done by a professional. That's when

Chapter 4 – Step 4: Creating Your Budget and Staying on Track

discouragement and frustration can put the brakes on an otherwise beautiful design idea.

Planning a budget for your interior design project is very important and will vary for everyone depending on material costs and construction labor if you have walls to remove or need a little helpful muscle for your home improvements. Knowing exactly how much money you have set aside helps you plan your project and stay on track when you're tempted to justify a more expensive purchase. It's so easy to fall in love with an expensive piece of furniture or some elaborate architectural changes and move forward when you can't afford it. Allowing yourself to max out your budget at the beginning of your design efforts can quickly leave you in a tight spot as you near the end.

Once you have decided on which rooms to include in your budget, it is time to start drawing up your final plan. The easiest way to do this is with a budget worksheet. Having a budget worksheet is an excellent way to refrain from spending more money than you have set aside. You can find many different budget worksheets online, or you can create your own.

Some of the items to keep in mind when creating your list of wants and needs are the following.

- Furniture
- What do you plan to use that you current own?
- What can be repurposed? Cost?
- What do you need to purchase?

Interior Design

- Fabrics
- Accents & Accessories
- Rugs
- Pillows
- Artwork
- Lighting
- Paint
- Wall Paper
- Crown Molding
- Window Coverings
- Architectural Features
- Cabinets
- Sinks/tubs
- Appliances
- Trim
- Flooring
- Closet Updates/shelving
- Construction
- Electrical
- Plumbing

Chapter 4 – Step 4: Creating Your Budget and Staying on Track

- Wall Removals/Additions
- Room Additions
- Permits
- Inspections
- Ceiling Fixtures
- Additional Doors
- Sales Taxes
- Delivery/Shipping Charges

Some suggested categories on your spreadsheet could look like this.

- Items
- Quantity
- Estimated Cost
- Estimated Tax
- Estimated Shipping
- Estimated Labor
- Total

Many newbies don't do a budget because it doesn't sound glamorous and fun, but creating a working budget will make your design job easier and much more successful. In fact, sticking to a budget can make or break your design efforts.

After completing your budget worksheet, it's a good idea to make a few copies of it so that you always have it on hand. Keep at least one copy in your car or wallet because it is important to have it with you whenever you go shopping for supplies. Now that you have your interior design budget, you can move on to the second step—determining the function of your rooms.

Chapter 5:

Step 5: Preparing to Decorate

So far, you have delved into your project to create a basic idea of what you want to do and determine your finances for the project. Now it's time to prioritize your tasks and then pull everything together to get the job done. There's that word "prioritize." This is one of the hardest things to do, especially when you're eager to jump in and see some results. As long as you've probably waited to do get started, resist the temptation to start buying your furniture and accent pieces. You've got some important work to do first.

An Overall Review

The first thing to do is create a notebook of design elements and furniture. Look through tons of design magazines, and each time you see something you like that suits your style, cut it out. Even if you think you could never afford anything like the item of your dreams, cut it out anyway. Divide your three-ring notebook into sections. Your sections should look like this, and then subdivided into the categories below each section.

Chapter 5—Step 5: Preparing to Decorate

- Art
  - Plaques
    - Pictures
    - Signature Pieces
    - Sculptures
- Rugs
  - Area
  - Throw
  - Carpeting
  - Hanging
- Furniture
  - Sofas
  - Chairs
- Bedroom
- Office
- Patio
- Tables
- Paint Colors
  - Gather Samples

- - o   Specific Colors for Rooms
  - o   Types of Paint
  - o   Paint Designs
- Accents
- Feature Pieces
- Fireplaces
- Wall Treatments
- Kitchen Cabinets
- Flooring
  - o   Vinyl
  - o   Tile
  - o   Wood
  - o   Marble
- Window Coverings
  - o   Drapes
  - o   Blinds
  - o   Shutters
  - o   Valances
  - o   Cornices

Chapter 5—Step 5: Preparing to Decorate

- Sinks/tubs
- Wall Paper
- Lighting
    - Living room
    - Kitchen
    - Pendant
    - Lamps
    - Artwork Lighting
    - Sconces

Place your cutouts on a white piece of paper backing so that you can clearly see the items. Leave yourself room to write on the paper to remind yourself what you liked about the item and where you were thinking of placing it in the home. Also, write "estimated cost" and leave a blank space beside it so that you can write in the cost after you have done some price shopping.

Don't focus on style right now, just create your notebook. You might surprise yourself with all the items and review them. The style you thought you wanted might not be represented by all the things you cut out for your ideas notebook. After you have spent some time finding all sorts of things you like, and your notebook is full, now it's time to examine your collection and prioritize the items.

Prioritizing Your Wants & Needs

Even if you have the money to do the entire design project at once, it's too overwhelming for a newbie to think in those terms. Like most projects, it's easier to know how to move forward when you take it in smaller steps and do your design in phases. Designing in phases can also be much more cost efficient, and you can enjoy your efforts on phase one while moving on to phase two.

When you're setting priorities, you can decide to do so by rooms, by project size or expense, or from easiest to most difficult. There are all different ways to prioritize, so take your choice. Whichever way you decide to prioritize your design, take one room at a time with most of it, unless it's flooring or paint. Even though painting and flooring are what you'll want to start on, you're not ready just yet. Before you begin picking out colors and deciding on flooring, you need to solidify your style, furniture, and accent pieces. For our discussion, we're going to give the living room a makeover; it will be the priority of our overall design project.

Taking a Personal Inventory

Once you know your style, examine the furniture you current have in your space. Ask yourself the following questions.

1. What furniture do I want to keep?

2. What furniture can I repurpose?

3. What furniture can I use in a different room?

4. What furniture should I ship to Goodwill?

Chapter 5—Step 5: Preparing to Decorate

Take a piece of graph paper and tape it to one of your white sheets from your ideas notebook. This will be your design drawing. The graph paper will enable you to draw your design with the correct spacing and dimensions. The drawing is just a starting point, but it will give you an idea of how you want to arrange the room.

Measure the windows, doors, hallways, stairs, pony walls, and any other item that is taking space in the room. Let each square on your graph paper represent six inches. So, if your room is 16 ft. by 16 ft., then you will pencil off 32 squares vertically and 32 squares horizontally—two squares equally one foot. These are the outside dimensions of your room. If you have a fireplace in the room that will remain the same size, mark that as well. So, these are the things you should have pre-marked on your graph paper.

- Windows
- Doors
- Fireplace (if any)
- Hallways
- Steps (if any)
- Alcoves (for television)

If your living space is open on one side, then leave that side open on your graph paper as well. If you have decided to keep any pieces in your living space, measure those you choose and temporarily place them in your design drawing. Again, every two squares should equal one foot. So, if you decide to keep your sofa and it's eight feet long, that would take up 16 squares on your graph paper. Include in your inventory what lamps, accents, and anything else you might want to use with your current furniture. Once you decide what you're keeping, look through your ideas book and determine what type of furniture would go with the pieces you are keeping. Place those sheets at the front of your notebook.

The furniture sheets in your notebook will be categorized in the first section, which will be titled new design. This section will include pictures of all those things that might be included in this design project. If you're not sure whether you are keeping a light fixture or if you're discarding it, then include pictures of light fixtures. Again, leave yourself room to put the price after you do your price shopping. The only thing you have on your design drawing are the things you are keeping in the room.

Time to Price Shop

This is not a buying trip; your only price shopping to see if all that you want will fit your budget. You can't purchase the furniture yet because you'll still need to get an idea of what fabric will cost, window coverings, paint, flooring, etc. So, take out your idea sheets for these items and put them in the front section of your notebook, along with the furniture. If you need to do architectural changes on construction changes, include those sheets as well just to remind you to price them out.

Since flooring will be your most permanent and probably one of the highest expenses of your design, begin price shopping for flooring. Avoid deciding on the flooring as yet, just price out the different types of flooring you want to consider. For example, price out several types of wood, and several tile samples, along with some vinyl flooring if you want to consider that option. When you shop for flooring, take notes and write down prices of all the different kinds you liked. Leave yourself

Chapter 5—Step 5: Preparing to Decorate

room to make compromises by pricing top of the line, medium grade, and lower cost flooring.

Go through each item on your sheets, always taking notes and writing down the estimated costs. Also, indicate whether the items you are pricing were new or used. If you choose to incorporate used items in your design, here are some of the places to look.

- Consignment Shops
- Moving/Yard/Garage Sales
- Craigslist
- Online Stores
- Neighborhood Blogs Classified Ads
- Model Homes Sales
- Designer Stores for Used Furniture
- Staging Company Sell Outs

Once you have priced everything, go back and see what best fits your budget. If you can't live without that top-of-the-line wood floor, then just know that you'll have to make concessions somewhere else to stay on budget. It might mean that you look for some used pieces or refurbish something of yours. Be sure to include the sheets on everything for the room, including artwork, rugs, and accent pieces.

If you have any architectural or construction needs, you'll need to get estimates on the work as well. Make sure you use licensed and bonded workers. Architectural and construction work is permanent, so you need it to be done right the first time. Also, don't forget to include installation and delivery costs. Use your budget worksheet and list all the items and their totals. Don't be disappointed when your first time around you end up way over budget on your preliminary wants. It's okay; you're far from being done with your planning.

Now that you know what you want, even when the price is over what you can afford, it's time to divide your wants from your needs. If you're working with limited funds, go middle of the road with everything when you are working through your pricing. Middle of the road with flooring, window coverings, furniture, art—everything except construction and architectural changes and labor. Leave yourself a cushion of money for the unexpected. Now, you should be under budget.

From here you begin to adjust your items by what you feel is most important. If the flooring is more important to you, then make that your higher priced design item. Do this until you are slightly under budget and have all the items you need as well as your reserve money. By now you should also have chosen what you want to use as a focal point because it's the focal point that you'll be emphasizing with your purchases. We're going to pretend that our fireplace is the focal point of the room.

From the Bottom Up Design

Beginning with your flooring--purchase it and figure your installation costs. Since our fireplace was the focal point of the room, we'll want to figure the cost of the changes up front. It's okay to be a bit elaborate on your focal point because it is what's going to get the most attention.

Chapter 5—Step 5: Preparing to Decorate

While you are waiting for the flooring to be installed, you can be shopping for your bigger pieces of furniture, and reupholster or repurposing any items you can to save money. Before you purchase items, measure them and draw them on your design sheet to make sure they will fit in the space. Take your notebook with you when you shop for furniture so you can first see the success of your design on paper.

Now that you've purchased the larger pieces, and decided on fabric, it's time to pick out paint colors and any wall moldings and window trims. Next, choose the ceiling fixtures, and then the lighting fixtures. Area rugs, artwork, and accent pieces can come later.

As you continue with your design, be constantly vigilant of your budget. Avoid going over budget and then running up your credit cards or taking out a loan. The added stress of overspending will create resentment about the project and any plans you might have for the next design project will dredge up those stressful memories.

Conclusion

If all this information hasn't dampened your spirits for beginning your DIY interior design project, you're ready to begin. You can get a head start by beginning to search through the magazines and developing a notebook of design items and ideas. This is the time to use your imagination and have fun, to let yourself dream as if money were no object. Experiment with creative ideas and open your mind to all the possibilities. Enjoy the honeymoon phase of your design; there will be time enough down the road to concern yourself with budget and compromises.

When you make the first part of your design exciting, it carries over to the next project and the next one after that. Experiences success after success encourages you to anticipate every new design challenge with eagerness. Each one will have its unique character and rewarding outcome. The beautiful thing about interior design is that with each project you begin with a clean canvas on which you pick the scene, colors, textures, and where you are going to place each piece.

It's true what they say that a picture is worth a thousand words. Be sure to take before, during, and after pictures of your interior design. Take pictures of the good times and the times you were pulling your hair out when something didn't show up on time or a design feature you know was going to look great wasn't quite what you expected. It's all a part of the

Conclusion

experience, and it will be fun to look back on each part of the design when you are done.

Another thing with pictures is that they remind you of small changes you'll make the next time when you move onto phase two of the plan. Think how much easier it will be in phase two. You'll already have your team of construction people, and you'll have items in your notebook. You'll know more about budgeting and the importance of sticking to one—that's for sure. You'll know what worked and what didn't with your focal point and paint colors. Most of all, the courage and confidence you gained from this experience will carry over to the next.

Before you begin, we wanted to thank you for downloading *Interior Design: The Best Beginner's Guide for Newbies*. We realize you have many choices of interior design books, and we appreciate you chose us to begin your design adventure. Keep this book close to you as you move through the design process. You'd be surprised at how many times it will come in handy when you need to review the steps or principles of design. When you need to re-evaluate decisions or figure your budget, you'll want to have us at your fingertips.

I hope this book has helped you find the peace of mind to begin your DIY interior design project. You're about to spend a significant amount of money and time working on your design, and we're happy to be a member of your trusted team. Our goal is to provide you with information that will not just get you started, but help you throughout your project and on to the next phase. When you complete your design, look around the space you created and remember when you were throwing your arms up in the air in confusion as to where to start.

The rewards are many; it's so self-satisfying to know that you can take an idea, apply the principles you have learned, and turn something worn and tired into something beautiful and vibrant. Each time you think you've come to an impasse, roll up your sleeves, take a deep breath, and find a new resolve to know that you are ready to tackle this thing. Every small step of success you find in your design builds your "I can do it" spirit. Who know, that spirit you develop in your interior design efforts might just follow you to other accomplishments as well.

The next step is to do what you been waiting for—jump on in and test your skills. Put your newfound knowledge to work. If you need a partner in crime, involve your significant other or best friend to join in the fun and excitement. Warn him or her ahead of time, though, that the need to create can become quite contagious. Once they see how well your design project turns out, they'll be soliciting you to help them with theirs.

Once you start working on your new design, you'll find yourself always keeping an eye open for things you can incorporate into your future projects. You'll be at a swap meet and find a unique piece to repurpose. Or, you'll find yourself becoming a regular at the upper-end consignment shops or antique stores. You'll get the design bug, and a few years from now when you look back at your first design efforts, you'll get a real kick out of your before, during, and after shots.

There's a reason why there are dozens of televisions programs on DIY design and home renovations. People have caught the design bug, and they have learned to turn their home into a showplace. If they can do it, you can do it, right? Now you can take the fun of watching into the excitement of doing the design yourself. If you're one of those who watches the

Conclusion

programs and thinks you could have done as good or better a job than the people on television, then it's time to give it a go.

What's your next step? Well, it's stepping into the room you are planning to change and start to think about what you want to do, what you'll keep and what you'll toss. Your next step is perhaps demolition day, or making your wish list. Your next step is to take your first step into the amazing world of interior design.

Finally, if you enjoyed this book, then we'd like to ask you for a favor. Would you be kind enough to leave a review for this book on Amazon? It would be greatly appreciated!

Thank you, and good luck on all your interior design projects!

Printed in Great Britain
by Amazon